Let's Talk About Rites of Passage, Deity and the Afterlife

Let's Talk About Rites of Passage, Deity and the Afterlife

Siusaidh Ceanadach

MOON
BOOKS

Winchester, UK
Washington, USA

First published by Moon Books, 2013
Moon Books is an imprint of John Hunt Publishing Ltd., Laurel House, Station Approach,
Alresford, Hants, SO24 9JH, UK
office1@jhpbooks.net
www.johnhuntpublishing.com
www.moon-books.net

For distributor details and how to order please visit the 'Ordering' section on our website.

Text and illustrations copyright: Siusaidh Ceanadach 2012

ISBN: 978 1 78099 945 6

A CIP catalogue record for this book is available from the British Library.

Design: Stuart Davies

Printed and bound by CPI Group (UK) Ltd, Croydon, CR0 4YY

We operate a distinctive and ethical publishing philosophy in all
areas of our business, from our global network of authors to
production and worldwide distribution.

CONTENTS

Acknowledgements

I would like to take this opportunity to thank Maria Moloney and Trevor Greenfield, both from O-Books, for their support in the development of this book and in bringing it to print.

The help that my daughter, Pauline Kennedy Allan, has given me while I have been writing this book and also with my previous books has been wonderful and I owe a great thanks to her. The continued support my husband, Piet Ceanadach, has given me has made this task so much easier.

I would also like to mention the forward thinking enthusiasm of the Pagan Federation and, in particular, Mike Stygal who continues to work towards providing material for children and their families to learn and understand more about the pagan faith. There have been two female writers over the years who have inspired me and still do; Vivienne Crowley, who's *Wicca: A Comprehensive Guide to the Old Religion in the Modern World* was the very first pagan book I read, and Emma Restall Orr, who continues to produce very good titles. Her little book called *Principles of Druidry* is well worth a read if you are new to a pagan path or interested in learning more about Druidry.

About Me

My name is Siusaidh Ceanadach and I have been a pagan since the 1980s. I was baptised and brought up in the Church of England and at one time was a very active member. I taught in Sunday School, ran house groups and my children were regular churchgoers. Then something happened in my life and I felt I could no longer belong to a group of people who no longer felt like my family; who did not give me the kind of support I felt I needed at a time when I needed it most. So I started to look around, thinking, 'There has to be more than this.' This led me to study astrology and this was followed by meeting up with teachers of Wicca. I trained in an Alexandrian Wiccan coven in London. After moving to Scotland I spent ten years working as a solo witch. I later found Scottish elders who took my training on in a more Gardnerian Wiccan way. My daughter Pauline introduced me to Druidry and I studied with the Order of Bards, Ovates and Druids, later becoming a member of The Druid Network.

I moved to Glasgow with my husband in 2001 and since then we have run a coven and a development circle. We co-ordinate ceremonies for all eight pagan festivals of the wheel of the year in Glasgow and run an open Druidcraft group called Tuatha de Bridget. Our group has people of all ages from babes in arms to those of venerable years. We have children who take small roles in our ceremonies along with their parents, and we encourage everyone to take part, even if it's just reading a poem or singing a song.

Introduction

I would like to say right from the very start that not all pagans hold exactly the same pagan beliefs, especially when it comes to deity. Some will see deity as a power within all of nature, a naturalistic approach. Some see a soul within animals. Not all will personify their gods at all, but I am writing this from my personal background in Wicca and Druidry, having spoken to many folk both in my own open pagan group and online.

If you look at a timeline of faiths, especially those affecting the British Isles, then you will notice some have been around since records began. There are those we can trace from around 1500BCE (BCE stands for 'before the common era' and means before the current system of numbering years) and faiths that seem to have come to a halt only to be taken up again in modern times. History books will have us believe that the all pagan religions died out and that what modern pagans follow is a mish-mash of things they have read in history books, fairy tales and stories that have grown from archaeology.

But there are pagan families who can trace their lines back for several centuries and during that time have conducted their own 'family rites' and followed their own codes, yet in outward appearances seemed to have been following the state religion. Whether state and religion should be intertwined is something I will leave to the reader to decide for themselves, or for teachers and classes to discuss. There have been times over the centuries that you either agreed to follow the religion of the state or you were killed, but thankfully these times have passed and we are now permitted to worship and hold whatever religious views we choose, most of the time without interference by the state.

In Britain we live on islands that have been invaded many times over the centuries. This has not always been something that caused bloodshed. In some cases peoples from other parts of the world have simply moved here and brought their own beliefs with them and told others about those beliefs. They may have married into local families and their children have followed either the mother's or father's faith, or maybe some aspects of both.

It is clear that the original inhabitants of the British Isles had their own faith, their own gods and their own festivals, and continued to celebrate these as the year turned.

When the Romans invaded Britain in the year 43CE, they started to build their long straight roads and their villas with baths and brought what they felt was civilisation. They also brought several religions. Why did they bring so many different beliefs with them? Because many of their soldiers were conscripts who came from other parts of the world and who already had their own faith. Thus early gods and goddesses who were worshiped here in Britain became a mix of the local spirits of place, early 'Earth Mother' and 'Father Hunter' figures and those brought into the country by peoples from other parts of the world. In the section of the book about gods I will talk a little bit about some of the different pagan gods that have been brought into Britain as well as touching on some of the other well known pantheons, or families, of gods. There will also be some activities to do and recipes to try. The second section of the book is about rites of passage, which are events that mark significant happenings in our lives. Lastly, I talk about what pagans believe happens after death.

Part One
Deity and Gods

Norse Influences

In the north west of England and up into Scotland there are many people who can trace their genetic roots back to Scandinavia, and these people brought knowledge and worship of the Norse gods to Britain.

The Norse came from Scandinavia, which includes Iceland, Sweden, Denmark and Norway. They had two families of gods. One family were sky gods known as the Aesir, who lived in a realm called Asgard. The Aesir were worshiped from 700BCE to 1100CE and, to an extent, they still are today.

The head of this family is Odin, the All Father. He has a consort, a wife, who is called Frigg. She has the title the Queen of Heaven. Have you heard that phrase before?

There is a Germanic version of the name of this goddess, 'Frija'. From her we get the word for a day of the week… *Friday.*

Another of the Norse gods who gave his name to a day of the week is Thor, the god of thunder and lightning who wields a huge hammer. From his name came Thor's day, which became the modern Thursday.

This family of gods had rivals, a group of gods called the Vanir, and the two fought a great battle.

Although these two groups were always at odds with each other, their main constant enemies were the frost giants.

A Story: Odin's Vine

Carl lived on the east coast of England, in Sunderland. The village he lived in was called Bishopswearmouth. In days gone by it had been a very small village, but it had become swallowed up by new developments of houses, factories, schools and colleges.

The house he lived in had been in his family for many generations, passed down from father to son. In each generation the oldest man, the grandfather, had taken care of a very old vine. The back garden was south facing and there had always been a glass house built onto the back wall of this large and rambling home. It was one of the roles of the grandfather of the family to tend this vine. It had a name, and it was called Odin's Vine.

It was said that many generations ago a strange man had appeared soon after a storm which produced a most wonderful rainbow. The man had worn a very large brimmed hat and he had a patch over his right eye. The Norse god Odin is described as only having one eye. The stranger also had a raven sitting on his shoulder and another one was flying around near him, just like the Norse god Odin is said to have. The man had asked for a drink and at that time the only safe thing left in the house to drink was a bottle of wine.

So, one of Carl's ancestors had given this strange man the bottle of wine. He produced a hollow horn drinking vessel, poured the wine into this and drank

7

nearly all of it. The strange man apparently emptied a tiny drop onto the ground and said he would call back from time to time for a drink.

From that drop grew a vine which bore grapes. These were tended by the oldest man in the family, the grandfather, and those grapes each year were made into wine. It was called Odin's Wine.

One day Carl went to find his grandfather, to ask him if there was anything he could do to help and whether it was time to harvest the grapes yet. But there was no answer when Carl knocked on his bedroom door, which was very strange because he was normally an early riser. Carl had expected his grandfather to call back 'come in'. After waiting for a while, off Carl went to find his mother who was down in the kitchen.

'Have you seen Grandfather this morning?' Carl asked.

'Come to think about it, no I haven't,' said his mother. 'Perhaps we need to see if he's just sleeping or if there is anything wrong.'

Right away, Carl's mother went up the stairs and along the corridor. She knocked on the door. There was no reply at all so she went in and found Carl's grandfather still in bed, very hot, mumbling words none of them could understand. Even when he opened his eyes he did not seem to recognise them.

'I'll call a doctor. He's clearly picked up some kind of infection which has put his temperature up, and he has a fever,' she said.

And just as she said that they both heard an eerie sound in the distance, was it a dog? What was it making that noise? Carl looked up at his mother and she looked down at him.

'Well if I didn't know better I would say that sounded like a wolf,' she said.

'I didn't think there were any wolves here in Britain,' said Carl.

'No, there are no wolves running wild here in Britain, but I still think that sounded like a wolf,' she said.

They both went quickly downstairs. Carl's mum went to the telephone to ring for a doctor and Carl went out into the garden to listen again, just in case he heard that sound, the howl!

The vine was full of grapes. It had not rained for about a week, so Carl's grandfather had been giving the vine a drink of water each morning and evening. Carl thought he should do this little job for his grandfather and so he went to fetch the watering can and filled it with water from the huge water butt that collected rainwater which ran off the roof. When he got back to the vine there was a huge black bird sitting on the vine. 'Shoo!' said Carl. 'Leave the grapes alone, these are Odin's grapes.' The bird made a strange croaking noise and flew off leaving one feather, which floated to the ground.

Carl finished the watering, put the watering can back in its place and collected the black feather to show his mother.

'This is from some huge black bird that was sitting on the vine,' Carl told his mother. She took the feather and looked at it very carefully.

'That's not from just any old black bird, it's far too long, I think it's from a raven,' she said.

Soon after that the doctor arrived and went upstairs to visit grandfather. Carl went back outside, just to see if there was anything else he could do to help the vine. It was a bit worrying that the doctor had to be called. Normally his grandfather was a very healthy man. The doctor prescribed some tablets for grandfather and said he needed plenty of bed rest.

The time passed quickly after the doctor left, with mother going up and down the stairs to nurse his grandfather and Carl doing little odd jobs in the garden that he felt would help. Then in the early evening his father came home and was told the whole story about the strange howling, the huge black bird that had been sitting on the vine in the garden and, naturally, all about his grandfather having a fever.

By the time they had finished telling father all about the day's happenings, it had started to rain. Then, all of a sudden, there was a crash of thunder.

'Well, that's Thor banging his hammer again,' said Carl's father in a very matter-of-fact manner, as if it was a normal day-to-day thing.

It rained for about an hour, which did mean Carl could leave the watering the garden that evening as nature had taken care of that job. Then, just as soon as the rain had started, it stopped and the sun came out again. Carl and his father went outside to see a most beautiful rainbow.

'Remind me again of the things you heard and saw today,' said Carl's father.

So Carl went over the basic facts – grandfather being unwell, a strange howl, and then a huge black bird sitting on the vine and now a rainstorm and the rainbow.

'I think I know what to do,' said Carl's father and he went off down into the cellar calling over his shoulder something about a bottle.

Grandfather was still tossing and turning in his bed, his temperature was still high, but because he hadn't really woken up properly he'd not been given any of the tablets the doctor had left. Apart from washing his face with a damp cloth and trying to give him little sips of water, grandfather was still not on the road to recovery and that worried Carl. It worried his parents as well. And if Carl's grandmother had not died several years ago, she too would have been very worried.

It was starting to get dark by the time everything was ready for what Carl's father has called 'a libation'. There was a bottle of wine made from grapes produced by the old vine several years ago, a horn drinking vessel and a corkscrew.

The little family gathered in the garden in front of the old vine and Carl's father opened the bottle with the corkscrew, next he poured the wine into the drinking horn and lifted it up towards the sky.

'Odin, All Father, I have a bottle of the best wine for you, come and take a drink,' he said. Then he turned the drinking vessel upside down and started to pour the wine onto the earth.

There was a strange croaking as two ravens flew into the garden and that made them jump and stop pouring the wine onto the ground. Then, as if from nowhere, a tall man appeared wearing a long coat that went right down to the ground and a very wide brimmed hat. When he lifted his bearded face up they all realised he was wearing a black patch over his right eye.

'I'll take that!' said the stranger. He grasped the drinking vessel, lifted it to his lips and drank everything left in the vessel!

'Good wine, keep making it and I'll be back from time to time for another drink,' said the man; and he was gone, just as quick as he had arrived.

The two black ravens flew with him and as he disappeared down the garden they all heard a wolf howl.

Grandfather, on the other hand, had missed all of this. He woke up to hear the call of the ravens and the howl of a distant wolf. He was hungry and thirsty and it wasn't long before he was on the road to recovery and back at his old job of looking after Odin's Vine.

Greek Influences

Ancient Greek speaking peoples who came to settle in Britain also brought their gods. Of these, the sky father is Zeus. He was the head of a large family of lesser deities who were all ruled by him. Zeus had a partner, a consort whose name is Hera. She is another Queen of Heaven. This family of deities were said to be universal in Greek mythology and all mortal sovereignty was said to come through Zeus.

The Ancient Greeks felt that the winds brought the change in the seasons. Boreas was the north wind and brought in the cold wind of winter. To the Ancient Greeks, those who lived in Britain were referred to as 'Hyperborean'. This meant people who lived behind the north wind.

Eurus was the east wind, and was the only one not associated with a season.

Notus, the south wind was the bringer of storms of late summer and autumn.

Zephurs came from the west and brought the light spring breezes and early summer.

Ancient Greek people would talk to the winds and they would make offerings to the spirits of the winds to ask for fair weather.

A Story: Miles in Athens

Ever since Miles' family had arrived for their holiday in Athens, the sky was overcast. It was warm, very warm and there had been very little rain for weeks, their host said, yet the sun did not shine.

Miles had been looking forward to this holiday for months. He had been looking into Ancient Greek gods for a project at school. They had chosen to come to Athens because his family had agreed that Athens was a lovely centre for making trips out to the islands and travelling around the nearby area. Athens is a very busy city, normally very hot, and the traffic is terrible with lots of traffic jams and a shortage of parking spaces – a situation only made worse by the heat.

No one knew for sure why the sky was so grey. Some said it was because of a volcano that had erupted and sent ash high into the sky and this had been blown around and seemed to have settled there. And there were some, especially some of the very elderly residents, who said it was because an ancient altar on the hills above Athens had been vandalised.

Several things were planned by Miles' family; a trip to the islands on a boat and a trip up into the hills above the city. The trip into the hills was to be led by a local scout leader called Pelos who was used to taking groups of people climbing and hiking.

It was another very grey day when the family was due to take the walk up into the hills and Miles was the only one who wanted to go. So Pelos led Miles on a long walk up into the hills above the city and they started to climb. They stopped at lunch time at a café which had tables out of doors and served cold drinks and ice cream. After a rest for refreshments, they started walking again, aiming to reach the summit.

They had been walking for about half an hour when they came to what Pelos said was a sacred altar to the old gods. All Miles could see was a broken flat stone, two smaller stones and an area of the hill that had been flattened a little.

'This is terrible, look at the damage,' said Pelos.

Miles did look, but he really couldn't see what the problem was. 'I don't see a problem unless you mean this broken flat stone,' said Miles.

'It is meant to be a single stone and this is where people leave their offerings for the old ones, the ancient gods. This one is to Hera, the wife of Zeus,' said Pelos.

'Why don't we look around for a new flat stone and put the whole thing back together?' asked Miles. Pelos gave him a very strange look, but agreed that would be the best idea, if it were possible.

So the two of them looked around and after a while found a flat stone to use for the altar, then they took the two uprights and bedded them into the soil to get them to sit firmly. Then they lifted the new stone into place and stood back to admire their work.

There was a sharp crack, the sound of someone stepping on a twig and they both looked round to find a woman with long fair hair, wearing some kind of kaftan tied in the middle with a fancy belt. The woman was leaning on a tall stick and she looked very hot, weary and dishevelled.

'Pardon, I did not intend to make you jump,' said the woman in perfect English.

'Can you spare me a drink of water and perhaps an apple?' she asked.

This was all very odd Miles and Pelos both thought, but they replied politely.

'We would be happy to help, but please can you just wait a few moments while we dedicate this new altar to Hera, the wife of Zeus?' said Pelos.

The woman smiled and nodded her head and waited, leaning on her tall wooden stick and Miles began...

'I dedicate this new altar in the honour of Hera the wife of Zeus, the Sky Father,' said Miles and sprinkled a little bit of water from his drinking bottle over the stone.

'Wonderful!' said the woman, and she cracked her stick onto the ground.

There was a rumble and a flash, then the grey clouds rolled away and the sun came out in all its glory. A fresh breeze picked up and the plants on the hill started to move in the gentle breeze.

As you can imagine Pelos and Miles jumped at the sudden noise and felt the electric atmosphere.

'Now may I have a drink of water and an apple?' asked the woman.

'Yes, have mine,' said Miles as he looked in astonishment at the strange woman. She seemed to have changed. Over the last few moments her hair had got smoother, as if someone had been up to comb it into place and she looked much smarter, in the kind of white long coat that the priests wore in the summer.

'Who are you?' asked Miles.

'My name, dear boy, is Hera! I have been unable to do very much at all until someone with a pure heart dedicated a new altar to my name,' she said.

'I'm glad you like it and we can write your name on it if you wish,' said Miles.

The woman smiled and looked down at the grey flat stone and on it was suddenly carved the words 'Hera and Zeus'.

'How did you do that?' said Miles.

'These things are all in the mind,' Hera said. 'It's just a matter of intent, of thinking very hard that this is what you wish and it can be done.'

'I must be off. Thank you for the new stone,' she said, and with that she was gone, just as quickly as she had arrived. Miles and Pelos both turned round to look at the new altar and there, still cut into the stone, were the names 'Hera and Zeus'.

Pelos rummaged in his backpack and pulled out another apple and went and put it carefully on the stone. 'Here you are my lady,' said Pelos and through the wind a voice was heard to say, 'Thank you Pelos! We will remember your kindness.'

Because of the fresh breeze that had helped blow the grey clouds away and the clear blue sky and the sunshine, the trip down the hill was much nicer. The two stopped on the way down to have a snack and a drink at the café on the hill and were greeted by many people telling them stories of how there had been a sudden cracking sound, a flash and then the grey clouds had rolled away and now there was beautiful weather.

'All we need now is a little light rain to lay the dust,' one of the people from the café said.

'Yes, a little light rain would be very nice,' said Pelos looking up into the sky. Almost before he had finished the sentence a drop of rain fell on his nose.

By the time they reached the bottom of the hill, people were laughing and dancing in the street, lifting their faces to a very gentle rain which came from light fluffy tiny little clouds that floated across the otherwise clear blue sky.

Pelos had just a few parting words as he left Miles with his family: 'Always remember the old ones and give them respect, you never know who you might meet.'

Miles knew he would have a lot to tell his class when he went back to school after the holidays and he especially wanted to tell them to show some respect for the ancient gods, for you never know who would come to your aid.

Recipe: Greek Salad

Ingredients for the salad

2 plum tomatoes, diced

1 1/2 English cucumbers, diced

1 red pepper, finely diced

3 tablespoons red onion, finely diced

1 cup pitted kalamata olives, whole or halved

2 tablespoons parsley, chopped

Ingredients for the dressing

3 tablespoons red wine vinegar

2 teaspoons Dijon mustard

2 teaspoons honey

1 teaspoon dried Italian seasoning

1/2 teaspoon salt

1/4 cup olive oil

To complete the Greek salad

1/2 cup feta cheese, crumbled

1 tablespoon parsley, chopped

Method

Place the diced tomatoes, cucumber, red pepper and red onion together in a large bowl. Fold in the olives and parsley and toss together (turn over between two spoons) until well mixed.

To make the dressing

Children should ask an adult to help them with this part.

Whisk the red wine vinegar, mustard, honey, Italian seasoning, salt and pepper together in a small bowl.

Slowly add the olive oil to the dressing, whisking constantly.

To finish and serve the salad

Pour a little dressing over the salad and toss to ensure all the vegetables are evenly coated. You can add a little more dressing if you want. Crumble the feta cheese on top, sprinkle with parsley and serve in a big bowl or divide into six portions and share with your friends.

Roman Influences

The Romans brought us many different gods and these also had a father and mother figure. Jupiter is the king of the Roman gods, and his wife or consort is Juno. A lot is known about the Roman gods because the ancient Romans wrote so much about their lives and their society and much of that information still survives today. For example, most people know about Venus, who is the Roman goddess of love and beauty. Minerva is the Roman goddess of wisdom and Mars is the Roman god of war.

But the Romans also gave those who live in Britain a special goddess, one who they felt was the 'genus loci' meaning the 'spirit of this land'. She is known as Britannia. There are famous songs and pictures of Britannia and she has even been depicted on the back of many British coins over the centuries. She is often shown carrying a trident and shield and wearing a centurion's helmet.

Perhaps you would like to do some research about Britannia?

Ancient Egypt

You can begin to see that over the centuries mankind has given different names to different groups of deities or gods as they see them and as they understand them.

Over 2,000 years ago, the people in Ancient Egypt also gave special names to their gods. A well known Egyptian mother goddess is Isis and her consort, her partner, is the god Osiris. Isis and Osiris were widely worshipped in Egypt. Her titles included the Queen of Heaven, Queen of the Seas and many others. Osiris was the warrior protector, the father figure, the god who gave men their feeling of strength, a deity they prayed to before battle.

Among the peoples who came to live in the British Isles there may well have also been those whose deities were the Egyptian gods. We can trace the worship of Egyptian gods back in time from before 3000BCE to 500CE. These days many modern pagans also have altars to Isis and Osiris in their homes and say prayers or give thanks to this family of gods.

A Story: The Incense Ana Made

Shelia had been meditating every few days for weeks. She sat in a comfortable chair, took some deep breaths and shut her eyes and relaxed. She always set an alarm to ring an hour after she started, to bring her back to the present time and place.

She had been having the same images in her meditation for days now, although she couldn't quite get them clear in her head. So before meditating one day, she decided from the start where this meditation would lead her.

One deep breath in and then out, and another in and then out and by the time she took the third deep breath Shelia was visualising the scene she expected to see.

She was walking along a dry dusty lane between what looked like very old ancient buildings. Sitting on the floor, in the dust, was a young girl. She was crying.

'Hello, what's your name? Why are you crying?' Shelia asked the girl.

'My name is Ana,' said the young girl. 'I can't get the recipe right and I'm going to be in bad trouble.'

'Do try and stop crying and tell me what this is all about, perhaps I can help you,' said Shelia.

So Ana began her story, 'I live and work in the Temple of Isis. She's the mother goddess and one of the most important goddesses in the area. I was chosen from my village several miles away here in Egypt to come and train as a priestess of Isis and I have been learning all the tasks that a priestess of Isis should know. For the last few weeks I have been in charge of making the incense which is burnt in our ceremonies and soon it will be a full moon and I need a new fresh recipe to prove that I can be of service to Isis.'

'What will happen to you if you can't complete this task?' asked Shelia.

Ana carried on to explain that she was only about half way through her training and she needed to prove herself each step of the way or she would be sent back to the village. There she would be set to work doing the worst possible tasks and no one would want to be her friend. She would be a failure!

'Take me with you and show me what you are doing, perhaps I can help,' said Shelia. So Ana took Shelia with her back to the Temple of Isis.

They walked down a long corridor that had the most wonderful paintings of different scenes in the daily life of the priestess, but they were painted sideways, as if the people who were the models had all turned to face forward and stand with their head and arms turned sideways. Rich brown colours, deep blue and amber looked back at them as they walked towards the room where the incense was made.

Ana opened the door. Inside on wooden tables were jars and jars of different dried gums from trees. Then there were bottles of dried petals and more still of spices.

In the middle of the room was a stone table and on this was a round metal pot in which was a piece of what looked like charcoal.

There was a large round stone bowl on the table and a pestle and mortar next to it for grinding things in.

Ana had a grey slate which she was marking with a small piece of chalk. She said, 'You see, it's nothing special, it will not lift the spirits of the senior priestess.'

Shelia had made mixtures of dried flowers and plants to have in a bowl indoors to make a nice smell so she knew a little bit about this sort of thing.

'Where are the oils?' asked Shelia

'What oils are you looking for?' Ana asked.

Shelia started to mix some ingredients. As she worked, she explained to Ana that the mixture needed to be at least 50 percent gums, that this would keep the whole mixture going and then you had to add flowers and seeds, spices and last of all you needed to add some essential oils. 'I think we should use frankincense oil,' said Shelia.

Ana walked over to the other side of the room and found a small bottle of oil.

They turned all the ingredients around in the big stone bowl and added the oil and mixed it all again.

'Now let's try some,' said Shelia. They lit the charcoal, which took a long time but eventually started to glow red, meaning it was hot enough. They put a spoonful of the incense mixture onto the glowing charcoal.

The smoke rose up into the room and filtered out into the hall outside. The smell was beautiful and quite different from anything Ana had made before. Ana and Shelia carefully wrote down the ingredients and called the mix 'Isis Full Moon Incense'.

No one heard the tall very regal priestess enter the room so they both were surprised when she spoke.

'You are Ana, one of my student priestesses are you not?' the priestess said.

'Yes Lady,' said Ana as she bent her head in reverence to the very senior and regal person.

It was clear at this point that the priestess did not seem to notice Shelia at all. She never looked at her or spoke to her.

'I can tell you have spiritual help, I can feel a presence and I am very pleased to see how far you have come on your training. You will be called into the senior student group at the next full moon,' said the senior priestess. Then she turned around and seemed to glide out through the door, she walked with such grace!

Here is the recipe that Ana and Shelia wrote onto the slate:

Four parts of benzoin gum
Two parts of gum Arabic
Two parts of frankincense gum
Two parts of rose petals (dried)
Two parts of sandalwood chips
One part of jasmine flowers
Ten drops of frankincense oil

Ana turned around to Shelia and hugged her. They were both so very happy and it never seemed at all strange.

'Will you come back and see me again?' asked Ana and Shelia promised that she would make a point of coming to find her, especially in the run up to the full moon.

'Just call my name and I will call back and that way you can find me,' said Ana.

They hugged again and just as they were giving each other a hug a bell went off, at first in the distance and Shelia felt herself being pulled back and back.

Shelia took a deep breath and reached out a hand to turn the alarm off, opened her eyes and looked around. She was back sitting in her comfortable chair in the sitting room and an hour had passed since she took those three deep breaths.

One of the first things she did was to go find a book from her collection all about Isis who was the Egyptian goddess of nature and magic, the mother of Horus and the wife of Osiris. All these ancient deities were worshipped over a wide area of the world at one time, her book told her. Then Shelia went to find a notebook and tried to remember the recipe for the incense, so she could make it again.

How to Make Isis Full Moon Incense

You will need

A glass or china bowl. Don't use a plastic one as the grains of the gum can scratch the surface of the plastic and make it unusable for other things.

A pestle and mortar, the kind you would use in the kitchen to grind spices.

Kitchen paper to cover your table.

Below are the ingredients that are mentioned in the story. Where it states 'one part' I suggest you make that one gram or double it, even treble it so you have the same amount of ingredients in balance.

Ingredients

Four parts of benzoin gum
Two parts of gum Arabic
Two parts of frankincense gum
Two parts of rose petals (dried)
Two parts of sandalwood chips
One part of jasmine flowers
Ten drops of frankincense oil

Method

Weigh all the gums first and mix together with a metal spoon. Put them into the mortar and crush them with the pestle and then tip all of this into the glass or china bowl. Then add the flowers and wood chips and again mix this round with a metal spoon. Then take your bottle of essential oil and count the drops into the mixture, dropping them in different areas in the bowl.

Now take your metal spoon and gently turn it all over and stir. Lastly take the pestle and crush the mixture together to make sure it's all blended well.

You will need to store this in glass jars and it's best left to mature for at least 24 hours, although there would be no harm done to try a tiny amount on a glowing charcoal.

This last bit must be done with the help of an adult, your teacher, your parents or guardians, do not attempt to light charcoal on your own. (It has an ingredient which makes it spark to start with and this can burn!)

Tip

If you or your teacher/parent/guardian does burn themselves, quickly put cold water over the burnt area, you have only 30 seconds to stop skin burning, so be very careful!

Ancient Ireland and Britain

In Ireland there was another family of gods or god-like people, the Dannans. According to the stories about them, they came with invasion into Ireland of a people who are now known as the Gaels. This family of gods had a mother goddess called Danu and her consort was Bilé. From this couple came a whole group of very well known deities. I think one of the best known is Brigit, the daughter of Danu and Bilé. She was adopted by the early Christians and became Saint Brigit, and is called by some 'Mary of the Gaels'.

Later, some of the Irish Gaels moved into parts of what is now Scotland. Although they were by that time Christian, they brought their old stories with them. Many of these tales of the old gods were woven into the land they moved into and now appear in Scottish tales as well as Irish, particularly in the Gaelic speaking areas of Scotland.

In early Welsh history we hear about another two major families of gods, the house of Don and the house of Llyr. Like the Dannans, these are sometimes thought of as humans with godlike abilities and are remembered as ancestors.

You can see there is a pattern appearing over and over again. People often saw their deities as being like a super-human family; a father and a mother with children and other family members who took on different roles.

A Story: Sarah and the Fox

Sarah sat on a log at the edge of the woods. She knew how lucky she was, her dad worked for the Forestry Commission and her family lived in a cottage in the middle of this woodland. The only downside to all of this was that she never had anyone to play with, apart from the animals. It was late summer. The days were still very sunny yet the nights had started to get chilly and the dark came far quicker than it had in the height of summer.

Everything was quiet, then suddenly there was a movement at the edge of the woods and the sound of twigs snapping just a few metres from where she sat. Sarah kept very still, guessing it was an animal. Sure enough a large red fox came into view. Her coat was glossy and her tail was bushy, she looked in the best of health.

The fox stared at Sarah for a few moments, then turned and walked into the woods and stopped again and turned around. It was as if the fox was trying to get Sarah to follow. Sarah looked up into the sky and made a rough estimate of the time.

Guessing she would have time for a walk before tea, she set off to follow the fox.

They walked for about half an hour with the fox stopping and turning around to make sure Sarah was following, which she was, very carefully. Then they came upon a clearing, a space where a few of the trees had been taken down and the sun had reached the grass. The whole area was a rich green with lots of wild flowers. Sarah sat down on the ground and waited quietly to see what the fox was going to do next.

A movement caught her eye and she looked across the clearing between the trees. A beautiful stag was standing under the shade of the trees. He was standing so very still that Sarah thought she was seeing things and rubbed her eyes to make sure. She only looked away for a moment and when she opened her eyes again there was a woman standing next to her.

'Don't be afraid,' said the woman. 'I'm not going to hurt you.'

This woman was a little strange because she was wearing a long dress, which seemed an odd thing to wear in the countryside, and she had long flowing red hair. It was bushy as well, as if the wind had blown through it and left it untidy.

'Who are you?' asked Sarah.

'My name is Danu,' said the woman. 'And I know you are Sarah.'

'Where did you come from? How do you know my name and what's happened to the fox that was here a few moments ago?' asked Sarah, so many questions spilling out of her mouth all at once.

'I have been here all the time, since you saw me when you were sitting on a log by the side of the wood,' said Danu.

'But all I saw was a fox,' said Sarah.

'Yes,' said Danu and smiled. She understood that we see only what we can understand and what the magical folk want us to see. Then she looked across the clearing to the place that the stag was standing.

Sarah followed her eyes and jumped in astonishment for where the stag had been there now stood a tall man, very strong and brown from the sun. He was wearing green, and both his trousers and his tunic were forest green!

'This is Herne,' said Danu. 'We are both here because we need your help and we can tell you care deeply for nature.'

Sarah recovered the shock of finding one moment she was with a fox and a stag and then shortly afterwards she was with two very special people, very different people. She thought for a moment she was dreaming, that she had fallen asleep on the log in the sunshine and this was just a dream so she pinched herself to make sure!

'Let us explain all of this to you,' said Herne.

They began to tell her what this was all about. Over on the other side of the forest where new trees were being planted and in an area where the trees were growing fast there was a problem which was just getting worse and worse. The trees were being planted far too close and the animals could not move easily around the forest. The birds found it difficult to fly through the trees and they could not easily build homes. The whole area was dark, black and lifeless and something needed to be done about it before the blackness crept through the forest. This darkness was attracting bad spirits, a great depression had grown, and was creeping like a claw into the area and no light or air was getting to the ground.

'But what can I do? I'm just a young girl,' said Sarah

'You were one of the only people we knew we could trust with this task and we will help you as much as we can with all of this,' said Danu.

Herne and Danu went on to explain how Sarah could help. They needed her to speak to her dad and get him to come with her to the other side of the forest and look at the trees, to walk into the dark and see for himself, but he needed to be very careful because anyone who stayed in that area for any length of time could be caught in the claws of the dark cold spirits. So he was to take a rope and tie one end onto his belt and the other end of the rope was to stay outside the dark area.

It took Sarah a few days to persuade her dad to come to this side of the forest and he was very wary about tying a rope onto his belt, but eventually he agreed, just to stop Sarah worrying so much.

There was a red fox in the area the day they went over to the black side of the forest, but she kept her distance. The trees and bushes rustled and when you looked into the bushes all you could see at a distance was a single stag grazing. There was no bird song, no sound of insects; apart from these two creatures all was strangely very quiet, depressingly quiet.

Sarah's dad had a measure with him and a torch, and he had a mobile phone although there was very little signal in that area. Off he went into the dark forest, further and further.

In a while the fox came to stand near to Sarah, and then the stag also came. Sarah looked down at the rope to see it was stretching out still and when she looked up both Danu and Herne were standing there with her. She jumped!

'I'll never get used to that,' she said. As she turned around again to look at the rope it had started to glow a warm orange, just enough light to follow, just enough light to keep any darkness away.

Sarah's dad never did find out to this day why or how his rope started to glow, but it was enough to follow back out of the darkness and back into the sunlight. He went back to his office in the cottage and made arrangements for the forest to be thinned out. Over half of the trees were taken out that autumn and the light came back. The animals were able to get back inside the forest and the birds started to use the remaining trees as homes.

And the black depressing spirit? It was banished far away, never to return! And Sarah continued to meet up with the fox and at times with the stag, for he was the very Lord of the Forest, the spirit of its life.

And Danu? She had come over from the land where her people lived in order to stop the death of the spirit of the forest, to save all the animals from the dark, bleak depression.

She's still around, just the other side of an invisible veil, in hearing yet not close enough to touch.

Herne, the Lord of the Forest, can be found often walking on the tops of the trees at very magical moments and sitting in the woodlands or in his guise as a stag grazing in the clearings.

Recipe: Colcannon

This is a traditional Irish dish. I am happy to say this recipe has been tried and tested by children and their mother, who suggested adding some bacon pieces.

Ingredients

1 kilo of potatoes – peeled, cooked and mashed
1 large curly leaf cabbage – chopped finely and cooked
1 large onion – chopped
10gms butter
5gms salt
Good sprinkle of pepper

Method

Wash, peel, and cook the potatoes in a saucepan by first putting them into cold water, bringing them to the boil and cooking them for about 20 minutes. When they are cooked, drain them through a colander and return them to the saucepan and mash them until they are soft and fluffy.

Wash, chop and cook the cabbage by putting it into boiling water for about ten minutes and then take it off the heat and strain all the water away.

Chop the onion and fry it in a little of the butter until the onion goes soft and changes colour, but don't fry it until it is brown!

Add the cooked cabbage and onion into the mashed potatoes, mix well and add salt and pepper.

Add in the butter and mix all the ingredients together.

This mix can be cooked in the oven in an ovenproof dish with a little butter on the top for about 20 minutes at a medium heat or you can simply dish it up with perhaps bacon, or fried eggs. Bacon and colcannon goes very well together.

Gods and Goddesses, Male and Female

There are many differences between the pagan faith and Christianity and between pagans and those of many other faiths. One of the biggest differences is in the way pagans see their gods, the different families they come from and the different areas they protect. Pagans often see their gods as both male and female, with the males, often father figures, having the strong fighting qualities of many of our heroes and the females having the caring, nurturing qualities of a mother. To be able to understand our divine parents the ancient peoples often gave them names and saw them as characters. Today modern pagans use many of the same names as people did in ancient times.

We might see the main male god as the Green Man or Herne the Hunter, or we see him as a father figure, Father Sky, if this helps with your understanding.

We see the main female goddess by general names, too, like Mother Earth, or simply as 'the Mother'. These are the most basic names which we talk about when learning about the male and female gods and goddesses. Let's go with 'Father Sky and Mother Earth' for the moment.

In Mother Earth we have the mother who grows food, trees and plants, and provides for our needs. In Father Sky we have the father who gives light and warmth and protects us and Mother Earth in order for all the wonderful things on earth to be grown. One would simply not work without the other, we need this balance of duality, the balance of male and female.

In the British Isles the people also had a Mother Goddess and Father God, and these were very much nature-based in very early times. We have already talked about Mother Earth and Father Sky, but early British tribes had named gods of their own.

One of the early powerful goddesses of the British Isles, whose protection extended all over Northern Europe right up to Finland and Norway, was someone we don't know a great deal about, although she is mentioned in a few ancient tales, especially in Wales. The modern name we have for her is 'Elen'. What she may have been called in ancient times we do not know. We speak of her as 'Elen of the Ways' but there are different variations of her name too such as Elaine, Helen and in some tales she is linked with a Saint Helen. She is associated with pathways, ley lines, roads and guiding people along a path. She is the powerful spirit of the Deer Women, because she was associated with deer, especially reindeer.

A Story: Elen and Santa's Grotto

The plane bumped a little as it came down through the clouds and then landed on the runway. All around through the window were just miles and miles of snow and yet everyone was going about their business. There were motor scooters drawing little trailers and they were all on skis. It had been a long day and they were looking forward to a nice hot meal and an early night.

The family had arrived by plane from London's Gatwick airport up to Glasgow airport and then all the way to Helsinki in Finland. From there they travelled north until they came to the hotel where they were booked into to stay. It was getting more and more exciting.

Tansy and George were twins. They were now nine years old and with midwinter approaching they had been looking forward to a winter holiday to beat all holidays. Since they were small their parents had been saying that one day we would all go to see Santa in the place where he was making toys and getting ready for the big winter celebration. After such a long time it had come, the holiday to see Santa.

Everyone at the hotel seemed to speak English yet chatted away to each other in their own language. The food was very different to the types of things Tansy and

George were used to, but it was well cooked, hot and had little strange dumplings with it. Mum had unpacked their clothes, dad lifted the case onto the top of a wooden wardrobe and by the time they came back from their evening meal the twins were more than ready to just drop into bed. They were tired and sleepy and looking forward to a trip the next day to visit Santa's Grotto!

While the twins slept, Mum and Dad tried a local drink, made plans for the next few days and then went to bed themselves. It had been such a long day and a very good one.

The next morning when they went down for breakfast their parents told them today's trip to Santa's Grotto was already fully booked and they had to book on one the day after, which was a bit of a disappointment. However, they would use the time to find all the warm clothes they needed, the snow suits, boots, hats and gloves.

So for the morning the family did just that. They went shopping and brought local clothes, and hats, boots and gloves and took them all back to the hotel.

After lunch the twins asked if they could go for a walk together.

'We won't go very far,' said Tansy.

'We'll take a torch,' said George.

So it was agreed and the hotel staff told them where they could go for a walk, so the twins, all dressed up in their snow suits, hats, gloves and, of course, their snow boots, set off.

It was dark. It never got light in Lapland during the winter, but people left little lights on at the front of their homes.

The two set off to walk through a very small wood and to do a wide circle round the hotel and all went well until the path split in two.

'Now which way?' asked Tansy.

'I don't know, do you?' said George.

'Oh help!' called Tansy. 'If anyone's hearing, please will you help us?'

A figure came walking down one of the paths and behind her the twins could see several reindeer. As the figure came closer they realised it was a woman, all dressed in reindeer skins, sewn together with large dark stitches. On her head she was wearing a hat which looked as if it had a pair of antlers attached to it.

'Maybe the reindeer follow her because she has antlers as well?' said George to Tansy.

When the woman first spoke neither of them could understand what she was saying and when they replied in English that they were lost, the woman took a moment and then started to speak in English.

'You are a little lost I think,' she said.

'We came out for a walk and don't know which path to take,' said Tansy.

'On a walk of discovery?' asked the woman and the twins nodded together.

'In that case I can help you. In fact I will lead you through the little woods if you wish,' said the woman.

'Thank you,' said the twins, together.

'My name is George and this is my sister, Tansy,' said George. 'What is your name, what shall we call you?'

'My name is Elen and I'm just the person you need to guide you along the path,' said the woman.

They all started to walk on with Elen leading the way and the reindeer following behind. They chatted away telling Elen all about their journey and their hope of seeing Santa. All the while they were talking their guide listened and nodded, as if she knew what they were telling her, as if she fully expected it.

As they walked they came to what looked a bit like a farmhouse, although it was difficult to tell with all the snow.

'We have to take the reindeer into the shelter, they need lots of rest at the moment,' said Elen.

And so the little group stopped. George and Tansy helped bring the reindeer into their shelter and helped feed them with dried hay and moss.

'Why do these reindeer need a lot of rest?' the children asked.

'Because very soon they will be eating magical mushrooms mixed with special moss in order for them to fly,' Elen said.

'But these are not Santa's reindeers, or are they?' asked George.

'Not exactly. They are and then again they are not!' said Elen.

So she started to tell the children about the reindeer. Each year they travel across magical pathways which you may have heard called 'ley lines'. These lines cross the world with high energy grids and the reindeer travel from one to another, the energy coming from the lines helps them travel very fast. They bring special magical gifts and wishes with them and answer messages left on trees and at cross-roads, so in one way they do bring presents although not the kind of thing you would expect.

'So if I asked for help with my school project, would they give it to me?' asked Tansy.

Elen drew herself up very tall, for she was a very powerful and magical woman.

'If I thought you needed special help and you asked for it, then yes it would be given,' said Elen.

'But what about Santa's reindeer? Where are they?' asked George.

And Elen went on to tell them that there were many reindeer kept in Finland and some of them would perhaps make the grade to become one of Santa's team. Each would be given the same name as the reindeer who had the job before them... the name went with the job. But normally Santa did not wear red and white, he wore green and brown. He had a warm hat but certainly not a red one!

She carried on to tell them that the red and white clothes that were worn over the

33

mid-winter season reflected the colour of the magic mushroom. These were red and white and when the reindeer ate the magic mushrooms they gained the ability to fly. But she gave them a warning, 'Never, ever touch these magic mushrooms, they can kill you. Only the reindeer can eat them without harm.'

After a while, she said, 'That's more than enough chatter, I think I had better get you back to your parents and if you come with me I will lead you down the right path back to the hotel where you are staying.'

And so it was that George and Tansy were taken back by the kind lady who wore antlers, and she left them a few metres away from the hotel. But when they got home and were eventually left on their own in the evening after dinner, George had something special to tell Tansy.

'You know the antlers on Elen's head,' said George.

'What about them?' asked Tansy.

'Well I can tell you now that no one is listening… they weren't in her hat, they were growing out of her head. Don't tell Mum and Dad because no one will ever believe us,' he said.

But we do, don't we?

Recipe: Norwegian Meatballs (Karbonader)

Ingredients

200gms of fine dry bread crumbs

125gms milk

500gms finely ground minced steak

1 egg, beaten

1 medium onion, grated or very finely chopped

2.5gms salt (half a teaspoon)

A small sprinkle of pepper

A good pinch to 2.5gms (half a teaspoon) of nutmeg

20gms olive oil

Method

Mix all the ingredients in a large bowl thoroughly and then shape into 24 little balls. Add the olive oil into a large sauté pan or frying pan and fry until the meatballs are brown all over and if you prick them, the juice runs clear.

Serve with gravy or simply stick wooden sticks into the balls and share them with your friends as a snack.

Part Two
Rites of Passage

Milestones in our Lives, Birth

Each human life is marked by special days. As we go through this journey of life, at each major step of the way our family and friends like to gather together to celebrate, or at the very least send a card, an email or text message to mark the occasion.

Our birth is the first happening in our life outside our mother's womb, the moment when we take the first breath all on our own. Life begins deep inside a mother's womb and grows for nine months. All this time we are nourished and fed by our mother through a cord that connects us to her. When we are born we start our independent journey, we take that first breath of life. In some cultures this date is written down and is called our birthday. We celebrate this date each year on the anniversary of our birth and, as we grow older, we have different celebrations to mark this special day.

Pagan families like to mark the birth of a baby with a celebration called a naming ceremony or a baby blessing. They invite family and friends and show the baby to all gathered. These events are often held out of doors and may require someone to conduct the ceremony. This can be a priestess and priest or a celebrant, or this can be done by a member of the family who has experience of this kind of ceremony. The baby is often dressed in something white or cream, perhaps a pretty dress or a very nice outfit that is special for the occasion. Often family and friends want to take photos to keep to remind them of this special day.

Pagans want the children in their care to be blessed by the deities, watched over by fairy folk and seen by departed ancestors, who are invited to join in the ceremony in spirit form. One of the main reasons to do all of this is to formally announce the baby's name, something they are going to be known as all through their life. A name can be a powerful thing.

Pagan folk to do not usually insist their children follow their own personal faith. Instead, they bring their children up to have an understanding of nature, some knowledge of paganism and other faiths, and try to give them a good moral code. When the children of pagan parents are old enough to decide for themselves, they can choose a spiritual path, a faith. Their parents would support them in this.

Although many pagan parents read their children stories about pagan mythology and talk to them about nature, they don't insist they follow the pagan faith nor do they make their children go through any ceremonies during their childhood years regarding joining the pagan faith. Nevertheless, children may be encouraged to come along to watch seasonal celebrations where that is possible. In closed Wiccan circles there is an age limit of 18 years before a person can be trained as a witch.

There are a few children who know from a very early age that they want to be pagan. They want to worship the old gods, they have a great love of nature, running around hugging trees and trying to talk to fairies. If my Druidcraft group finds a child who is desperate to be pagan and who understands what this means, then we welcome them along with their parents to our open gatherings.

There are also young people who are not sure if they want to be pagan, but are curious to find out more. Again these young people are welcomed at open gatherings with their parents, just as a curious adult would be. Pagans present do their best to answer any questions they may have about the pagan faith. However, they still are not able to train in any of the closed groups until they are 18 years old.

It's quite normal for children to go through stages of wanting to hug trees, and in some cases it's simply a stage of development. A great deal of comfort can come from being out in the fresh air and able to hug a tree.

All our growing years we have birthdays and there are other rites of passage we go through. In Victorian times all children had long hair and wore dresses! Then when a boy got out of nappies and became a child he had his hair cut for the first time and was dressed in short trousers and shirts. For many years small boys wore shorts to school and at home as well as on the games pitch. Then they reached a time when they started to become young men and they were given long trousers for the first time. Even today in some schools the younger boys all have shorts until they reach the top of the junior school when they are allowed to wear long trousers.

Little girls wore short skirts and had long hair in Victorian times until the day came when their mothers knew they had become young ladies and their skirts were lengthened and their hair was put up on their head. In those days it was not considered a good thing for a young woman to have long loose hair.

But these days little girls sometimes want to have their hair cut short and be free to wear shorts or leggings or skirts. There is no right or wrong way to dress. Some religions insist that when a girl reaches the point she becomes a young woman that she covers her head and doesn't show any skin on her arms or legs. There are also religions where the boys, once they reach a certain age, have to wear special head coverings especially in their places of worship.

What do you think pagan children wear? The answer is anything at all that they feel comfortable in, that keeps them warm in winter and that keeps them cool in summer, providing their parents allow it.

A lot of pagan families tend to dress in natural fibres such as cotton, linen or wool, but there are no restrictions about what materials they can use for clothes. They can wear bright colours, patterns or plain. Even at a spiritual gathering not everyone wears a special robe or a cloak. Some folk simply come in practical clothes, especially if it is an outdoor event, or wear something that makes them feel special.

A Story: Euan and his Sibling

Euan was going to have a baby sister or a brother, his mum Janet was expecting a baby very soon and her tummy had been getting bigger and bigger.

Euan's family lived on a farm in the countryside, about a mile from the sea if you could travel in a straight line, but much further than that by road. The farm was in a village up in the hills. There was a very twisty road down the hill and then a very busy road to the coast. Once you got as far as the coast road then it was about another hour's drive to the hospital and the maternity ward.

Euan's dad was not in the slightest worried. All his cows had calves and the ewes all had baby lambs each year. As far as he was concerned a baby was just another new life. Nothing to worry about at all, just nature, he kept telling Euan.

The midwife, however, was not feeling so easy about this. She lived about half an hour away in the next village and she knew that if she needed a doctor to help with the delivery, then it would be very difficult to get mother to the hospital safely, in time for the baby to be born in the maternity ward instead of at home.

Then one morning Euan came down to breakfast to find his mum walking up and down the kitchen, panting and holding her tummy.

'Is the baby on its way?' he asked.

'Yes, I think it is really time for the baby to be born today, but not yet, it will be a few hours before he or she arrives,' she said.

Euan's dad was away at the other end of the farm checking the cows and the sheep. He had left much earlier, before Euan was awake. So that morning it was just the two of them, Euan and his mum Janet.

'Can I do anything to help?' asked Euan.

'Nothing at the moment, just a matter of waiting now,' said Mum.

So Janet spent the rest of the morning walking up and down the kitchen, then sitting down and resting and Euan went to tidy his room and play quietly while they waited.

At lunch time Euan's dad came back to the house and heard the news that the baby was on its way.

'Right, I will go and fetch the midwife,' said Dad.

The midwife arrived quickly and went upstairs with Janet. Euan and his dad just waited and waited downstairs. Euan was worried they would have to go to the hospital to fetch the doctor.

About tea time they heard a scream from Janet. Euan and his dad ran up the stairs two at a time. When they reached the bedroom door, they heard the cry of a tiny new born baby. Janet and her baby were fine.

'It's a little girl,' said the midwife. 'Just give me about a quarter of an hour to tidy up and you can both come in.'

What a very sweet, tiny little thing she was, tiny little fingers and toes, Euan counted them and there were ten of each.

They called the new baby Heather and the little family settled down very quickly into a new routine. Little Heather needed to be fed every few hours, and her nappy changed. Euan got to hold her and rub her back. Sometimes Heather was a tiny bit sick on him, but it was only a little bit of milk and wiped off easily.

Heather was six weeks old when mum and dad told Euan that they would be having some friends and family round. They asked a celebrant – a lady who performed special ceremonies – to come to bless the baby and name her.

'She's already got a name, why does she need another one?' asked Euan.

Janet explained that as she and Dad were pagan it was their custom to celebrate the birth of a baby by holding a naming ceremony and having the baby blessed. Then all the guests were going to drink a toast of mead (which is a special drink made of honey) and have some food.

'Sounds like a party to me, and I like parties,' said Euan.

About three weeks later grandma and granddad came to stay for the weekend. Friends of mum and dad came along, including many pagans, and some of the neighbours too.

They all went into the garden. Dad had cut the grass and tidied it all up and the celebrant, who turned out to be a middle aged very plump lady with a nice smile, explained what was going to happen.

This is what she said: 'This kind of ceremony is normally, but not always, held out of doors. We are going to bless the garden and ask that it is made a sacred and holy area for the ceremony. Then we are going to speak to the spirit of the elements, to the air, the fire, the water and to the earth, ask them to join us and bless us.

'After that we shall ask our ancestors to join us in spirit, these are people who are connected to us by blood, line and place. This means our great-grandparents, our great-great-grandparents and all our family who have lived and died many years ago and it also includes everyone who connects to these people by marriage and adoption. The other ancestors are people who lived here many years ago, people who farmed these lands, but who died ages and ages ago.

'When everyone is here, then we will ask all their blessings and the love and blessings of our Goddess and our God, our spiritual Mother and Father.'

'Is the place going to be filled with ghosts?' Euan asked his Dad.

'No, not at all, we are asking their spirits to come,' he said.

It was quite an interesting little ceremony. Everyone was quiet and listened and the celebrant said prayers for Heather and the family. Then she took out a tiny bottle of oil from her pocket and dabbed a bit on Heather's head. She smelt very nice after that, of roses and lavender.

No one except Euan seemed to notice the other people who came along, all very well dressed for the occasion. They nodded and smiled at Euan and because he thought they were friends of Mum and Dad he smiled back at them all. After the ceremony Euan went looking for some of them, they were such a nice friendly bunch, but he never found them. So Euan went to talk to the celebrant and he asked her where they were.

'Ah! So you saw them too did you?' asked the celebrant. 'They were your family ancestors. We asked them to come and they came in spirit form, but some people can either feel them, see them or some can hear them. When you grow up you may not always be able to see and hear them, only a few folk keep this kind of gift, you are a very lucky and a very blessed boy.'

Euan understood and felt so much happier to know that his ancestors who had gone from this life still had another kind of life, a spiritual one, and that they would come and visit if invited.

'Shame the ancestors can't eat this cake,' he muttered to himself as he munched happily on Heather's Naming Cake.

Partnership, Marriage, Handfasting and Blessings

One of the major milestones in the most people's lives is the day they are joined with another. It may be a marriage, it could be a handfasting, a civil partnership or a blessing. It's a very special day in the lives of a couple who have chosen to spend a large amount of their time together. Couples in some faiths will marry 'until death us do part,' which simply means that they will stay together, regardless of what happens, until one of them dies. Then, and only then, would they choose another. The majority of pagan folk, if asked, will see this as meaning 'as long as love lasts'. They understand that it's possible that as people grow older, take on different jobs, develop different interests and perhaps different faiths, they can drift apart, eventually splitting up and separating. Happily the majority do form very long-term partnerships, often for life.

It is possible now in Scotland to have a legal pagan marriage, but in England and in Wales those wanting to get married would still need to go first to a registry office and have a legal ceremony, then go on to have a spiritual ceremony, often called a 'handfasting'. This very special ceremony asks a blessing of deity, ancestors, friends and family. It's very much a public declaration that two people wish to be known as a partnership, a couple. This can be performed for any gender, most often between two people, but it could also be celebrated between more than two. It's not legal to have a partnership with any more than two people in Britain, but there are no rules to say that perhaps three or even four could not be blessed together.

There are couples who choose to have a child and then decide to get married, then go one step further and want a marriage ceremony and a baby naming all at the same time. There are even some who have been together for many years and don't see the point of holding any kind of ceremony, they simply refer to each other as their 'partner'. But even here, the day they sign a joint mortgage or the day they move in together becomes a day they go on to celebrate and remember.

Separation and Divorce

As with all friendships, partnerships, marriages and romantic relationships, there is always a possibility that problems could occur. If they are not resolved, the couple could split up and go their own ways. The whole process may take several years as the couple try at first to sort their differences out and, if that doesn't work, then they might agree to separate. One normally moves out of the home, or in some cases a partner just leaves.

As you can imagine, all this can be very stressful, for the couple themselves, for any children they may have and the extended family. If the couple own their own home and have a joint mortgage – which means they borrowed money to buy the house and are paying that back – then all this becomes very difficult financially too. Normally it takes a solicitor to sort this kind of thing out and then it would perhaps need to go to the court for a magistrate to decide who pays what and when.

As a child I experienced this. I was seven when my mother told me we were going away to stay with an auntie. At the time I didn't understand that would mean I would never see my own home again and hardly ever see my father again. I spent several years with my mum going from one relative to another until we managed to get a little flat together. My father became known by his first name 'Freddy' and for a while I didn't have a dad at all. I'm telling you this because it all came right. My mum married again and her new husband became my 'Dad' and he was the best kind of dad I could ever have because he chose to become my dad. And sometimes when people make a choice to take on this role and become our parents they are clearly very special people.

So, when parents split up, as some do, it is very stressful. At the time it's difficult to know what is going to happen, but we do always have someone we can talk to, a teacher, a grandparent, an aunt or uncle, maybe a social worker, or perhaps the leader of our spiritual group, a Druid, a priest or priestess, or a minister. It's always a very good idea to talk to someone when we are feeling unhappy.

A Story: Ruth's Rose Petals

Things were getting exciting – in just three weeks Ruth's Aunt Sarah was getting married. It was not going to be in a church, or in any other building for that matter, because Sarah was a Druid! So was the young man she was going to marry, Bob. They had met each other when they went to a camp. They had sat under the stars, sung songs, shared some mead and listened to stories that other members of the grove had written and told to the gathering. Day by day over the week of the camp they had fallen in love and now, almost two years later, they were going to be married.

Ruth was going to be a flower girl. She was going to sprinkle the circle with red rose petals. She and her mum had been saving petals from the roses in the garden and in the gardens of all their neighbours. They had dried them very carefully on some kitchen paper in the warm.

It seemed like a long time ago that Sarah and Bob had come to talk to her family, to tell them that they were going to be married, but it was not going to be the kind of ceremony any of them was used to. It all sounded great fun! It was outdoors but they were going to have a big tent, just in case it rained. They were having a bonfire in the evening and a folk band were coming to play and sing. There was even a drummer coming along to the ceremony, although why you would have a drummer and not the rest of the band was something Ruth had not worked out as yet.

The dresses were made. Ruth had a long white dress a little bit like Sarah's dress, but hers had a ribbon around the waist. Their hair was going to be loose and they were going to wear circlets of little flowers. They both had new sandals, flat ones, because Sarah has said it was pointless trying to wear heels on the grass.

The time went very quickly and the day arrived, the celebrant turned out to be a very nice man who said he was 'independent'. He was some kind of a minister for pagan folk, although he would actually work for anyone who needed his services.

All the guests gathered together in the field where the wedding was taking place. The huge tent stood close by but today the sun shone and the sky was blue.

The celebrant told them all what was going to happen and asked everyone to stand in a big circle. Then Ruth went ahead of Sarah and sprinkled rose petals all around the circle and in front of the path she would take. The drummer marked a cheerful beat with his drum and in a few moments everyone was standing in the circle and the celebrant began.

'Spirits of the air, the fire, the water and the earth come join us now to witness this handfasting,' he said and all at once a wind blew across the circle and everyone hung on to their papers and their hats.

It stopped as soon as it started, in seconds, and was followed by a few drops of rain, but when you looked up into the clear blue sky, there was no sign of a cloud. The sun was hot and yet there was a strange rumble deep down inside the earth, people in the circle looked at each other, but the celebrant carried on as if it was all perfectly normal and he had fully expected the elements to respond. He had invited them, and they had arrived.

'Ancestors of our line, blood and place, come join us to witness this ceremony,' said the celebrant.

There was what sounded like footsteps, a rustle and it started to feel so much warmer. The celebrant smiled and nodded his head as if he was greeting someone.

'Let us welcome our Mother and Father, our spiritual parents,' continued the celebrant and everyone replied, 'Welcome Mother. Welcome Father.'

Later in the ceremony, Sarah and Bob read out words they had written to each other, things they promised to do for each other. They promised to be a support, a comfort and a shield and other things that Ruth could not remember afterwards.

Then came a strange bit, Sarah and Bob had their wrists tied together with cord. Then, with their hands still tied together, they jumped over a large broom made of twigs and branches. But everyone laughed and clapped and soon the ceremony came to an end.

The drummer set up a lively beat and folks started to clap in time. Then one of the guests started to sing and everyone who knew the song joined in.

'Before we go,' said the celebrant, 'we need to thank all those both seen and unseen who have joined us and say goodbye to them.' Everyone become much quieter as the celebrant went on.

'Mother Goddess, Father God, we thank you for joining us today in our ceremony, go with our love and thank you.'

Everyone replied, 'Thank you!'

'Spirits of the earth, the water, the fire and the air, we felt you with us and we thank you for your blessing,' said the celebrant.

'Thank you,' everyone responded again.

Then there was a rumble under the ground, as if they were all standing over the top of an underground train line and felt the train go past, it was a very odd feeling. Then a few drops of rain fell down and everyone looked up to the sky, and yet there were no clouds to be seen at all. In fact the sun seemed all of a sudden so much hotter and just as Ruth felt very warm the breeze blew her dress right up over her face! But she was not the only one, one or two of the guests lost their hats. Sarah's veil, which had been attached to the back of her dress, blew up and over her face.

Everyone laughed and then started to clap and the breeze settled down to a very gentle breath across the grass.

Then the ceremony was over, so much fun and quite different from anything that anyone else had been to before, apart from Sarah and Bob who had been to two or three handfastings.

Ruth was certainly going to remember this day for a very long time, the sunshine, the wind which came all of a sudden, the drummer, the laughter and the fun. But the day was not over because the band turned up soon after the ceremony and set up their things in the big tent. After a while they started to play. The food was set up on tables at the back of the tent and everyone helped themselves. Eventually, as it got darker, someone put a light to the bonfire. Many of the older guests went home and that left many of Sarah and Bob's pals from their Druid grove and Ruth, who had been allowed to stay up. The last thing she remembered was falling asleep on a rug in front of the bonfire listening to the beautiful songs everyone was singing.

Special Occasion Fruit Cake

Children will need an adult to help with this.

Ingredients

250gms butter, softened and beaten until creamy
250gms soft brown sugar
4 large or 6 small eggs
500gms self-raising flour
150gms sultanas
150gms raisins
150gms currents
2 to 3 teaspoons mixed spice
1/2 teaspoon of salt
Milk if needed to moisten
A round medium sized cake tin, or a heatproof silicone cake mould
Optionally, you could use 450gms of washed mixed dried fruit instead of the sultanas, raisins and currents

Method

Place the butter in a large bowl and beat it with a wooden spoon until it is very soft and fluffy, children can ask an adult to help using a food mixer with this part.

When the sugar is soft, add in the soft brown sugar and beat together until it is fully blended.

Crack the eggs into a separate bowl and beat them with a fork until all the yolk is blended with the white, then add some of the egg mixture, little by little to the butter and sugar. Beat it at every stage until the egg is blended into the butter and sugar.

At this stage the mixture should be thick and creamy and very soft.

In a large bowl put all the fruit. Add just a tiny bit of the flour to the fruit and fold it over so the flour coats the fruit, this helps to stop the fruit sinking. Put the floured fruit to one side.

Now add the flour, mixed spice and salt together into the creamy butter, sugar and egg mix. Do this little by little and fold it in with a metal spoon very carefully. At this stage try not to stir fiercely!

Once the flour is all added, add the fruit about a quarter at a time. Again carefully fold the mixture together until all the ingredients are blended.

Here's the fun bit, take a wooden spoon, fill it with a large amount of cake mixture and hold it over the bowl and start to count... one... two... three. If your mixture falls off the spoon before it gets to three, then it's too wet and may need a little more flour. Children should ask an adult to do this.

If the mixture does not fall off the spoon until perhaps five or six, it's too dry and needs a little milk.

Again this is something an adult will need to do, just to make sure you do not overdo the amount.

Put all the cake mixture into a cake tin and smooth it over. If possible put a dip in the middle. This should be just a very slight dip to help the cake rise evenly while cooking.

Heat the oven to 160c and cook at that temperature for the first hour, then reduce to 130c for a further hour, although it is best to check with the oven instructions for the best heat for a fruit cake first.

Check the cake after about half an hour. If the edges seem to be cooking far more quickly than the centre, then ask the adult helper to reduce the heat slightly.

The cake is cooked when you prick the middle with a fine knitting needle or metal skewer and it comes out clear. If the needle or skewer is marked with moist cake mixture, then it needs further cooking.

Take the cake out of the oven when cooked and leave it to stand for at least half an hour before attempting to take the cake out of the tin.

Leave it to cool on a wire rack or perhaps the wire from the grill pan until it is completely cool before starting to decorate it or cut it into portions to eat.

To decorate the cake, you can buy readymade marzipan and readymade icing that you can roll over the top. This will give you a plain surface. You can then write a name on it in icing sugar or decorate the cake with patterns such as stars and moons.

A Handfasting Play for Children to Perform

Characters in the play

Elder – to speak to everyone at the start and at the end, this should be a teacher or a Parent/guardian

Bride

Groom

Flower girls and boys

Celebrant

Spirits of Air

Spirits of Fire

Spirits of Water

Spirits of Earth

Mother Goddess

Father God

White Spirit called Awen, who is venerated by Druids

Guests: these can be children from different classes or groups who come to watch

Props required

You will need some ribbon or cord and a broom, the type you sweep up leaves with, made of twigs tied round a central branch.

You will also need crepe paper in yellow, red, blue and green and some in white.

The play

Elder: Welcome everyone. Today we are going to have a wedding, a pagan wedding, which is often called a handfasting.

Celebrant: We are going to welcome the spirits of the elements, so will you all say, 'Welcome air spirits'.

All: Welcome air spirits!

(*The air spirits, who have lots of strips of yellow crepe paper attached to their arms, run around the circle in a clockwise direction waving their arms so all the yellow shows well, the air spirits go and stand in the east.*)

Celebrant: Let us welcome the fire spirits, please repeat after me, 'Welcome fire spirits'.

All: Welcome fire spirits!

(*The group of children who are the fire spirits have strips of red crepe paper attached to their arms and run round around the circle in a clockwise direction, then go to stand*)

in the south.)

Celebrant: Let us now welcome the water spirits! Please say after me, 'Welcome water spirits'.

All: Welcome water spirits!

(The children who are the water spirits have blue streamers of crepe paper on their arms. They wave their arms and make the streamers look like waves and run round around the circle in a clockwise direction and then go to stand in the west.)

Celebrant: Let us now welcome the earth spirits. Please say after me, 'Welcome earth spirits'.

All: Welcome earth spirits!

(The children who are the earth spirits have green streamers of crepe paper on their arms. They wave their arms and stomp around the circle in a clockwise direction in a heavy-footed way like gnomes. They go and stand in the north.)

Celebrant: Let us now welcome the Mother Goddess and the Father God.

(This couple do not need to do very much other than come into the circle and stand. They can be dressed in green and, if possible, the Father God could have a Green Man mask or green leaves painted on his face. The Mother Goddess could have a silver mask or have a moon and stars painted on her face.)

Celebrant: Can we now have the bride and groom into the circle.

(The bride and groom walk into the circle and go to stand in the centre facing the celebrant.)

Celebrant: And now that we are all gathered, we ask that the Spirit of Awen come and join us.

(The Awen, dressed in white, with white crepe streamers, runs all around the circle, outside or behind everyone, and then comes to stand in the circle and watches.)

Celebrant: Please can we have the ribbon which will bind the bride and groom?

(Someone brings a ribbon, about three metres long, which could have been braided with other colours or even with sparkly material, into the circle and gives it to the celebrant.)

Celebrant (to the bride and groom): Do you wish to be bound to each other?

Bride and Groom together: Yes!

(The celebrant hands his or her book to the nearest person to hold and, with both hands, winds the ribbon around one wrist of the bride to one wrist of the groom.)

Celebrant: Who has the broom?

(Someone brings a broom decorated with ribbons. It is held by the celebrant and one other person just a few centimetres above the ground. The bride and groom now jump over the broom with their hands still tied.)

Celebrant: You are now handfasted, congratulations!

All: Congratulations! Well done! (Clapping by all.)

(Teachers/parents/guardians may want to get all the children to wave goodbye and run around the circle in an anti-clockwise direction and off into another area at the end of the

little play or, alternatively, they could all take a bow and then wave goodbye.

The class can now say their thanks to everyone for coming along to see their wedding and snacks and refreshments could be shared.

Note to teachers and guardians in the southern hemisphere

If you live in the southern hemisphere then you will need to change the directions of the elements and you may also wish to change the direction the children run.

Passing, Death and Funerals

One thing is for sure, every one of us will eventually die. We all hope this will come when we are very old. With old age people are sometimes less able to do all the things they want to do and sometimes old age brings poor health. We hope that when our time comes we are going to be ready for the next stage, but sadly this is not always the case. Some people, even children, do die well before they and their family would want them to.

As a pagan and from a pagan point of view I want to say that this is very sad for us and we do all feel grief as badly as any other human being, but the fact that we believe in a life after death does help a little.

We believe that at death a person's spirit, the essence and energy part of them, leaves its body, becomes a separate entity and travels on. What we see after a person has died is simply a kind of overcoat, a flesh and bones container that our spirit has lived in and with during its lifetime.

The feeling of great sadness, the empty feelings of the friends and relatives of the person who has died, are all part of something we call 'grief' and it's very normal and natural to have these feelings. In fact, you would not be human if you did not feel something when someone you knew died and passed on. I am not going to tell you the cure for these feelings, I am not even sure there is a 'cure' as such, but having lost members of my own family I can tell you that all the feelings I have now are not nearly as terrible as they were the day they died.

Little by little you learn to adjust and learn to carry on without that person in your life, at your school, on the other end of a phone call.

It helps to talk with people who understand how this all feels, other family members, friends who have had these experiences or perhaps counsellors. So if you are reading this, whether you are young or old, and you have lost a member of the family, a friend or even a neighbour, if you have had a death which has made you feel very sad, lost and lonely, you would feel better if you talked to someone who understands. That someone may perhaps work as a counsellor or might be your teacher or a member of your family. It's not a cure, it will never make the hurt go away, but little by little it will help you come to terms with all of this yourself and understand how this has made you feel.

When someone dies a doctor is called to make certain the person is not in a very deep coma, and that the person has indeed died. The doctor has to fill in something called a 'death certificate' and then the head of the family has to take this certificate to a registrar to have all the details filed in a registry. The registrar issues some forms, which the head of the family takes to an undertaker who can then help arrange the passing rite, the funeral. The body of the person who has died is then collected from their home or the hospital and taken to a place often called a chapel of rest. There they are washed and dressed ready for their final ceremony. You will probably already know that people who have died are usually put in a special box or casket called a coffin.

There are all kinds of coffins available. Many of them are made of wood but these day it is increasingly common to find coffins made of other materials, including hard thick cardboard, basket-woven materials and many different kinds of things that are bio-degradable, which means they will return to the earth easily. As many people are not buried but cremated these days, perhaps one way in which we can save the trees and the planet is by choosing material which is easier to replace than solid wood. I like the idea of a willow casket, something made from material which grows very quickly and can be easily found.

But we have to remember how other people feel about all of this and many still feel that people should be buried in wooden coffins. Not everyone can cope with trying to make their mind up about this kind of thing, especially after they have just lost a member of their family or a close friend. So maybe, difficult though this subject is, it is a good idea to talk about things like this while someone is alive and well.

So the day comes when the ceremony to say goodbye or bid farewell to your loved one arrives. This is normally about a week after their death. Anyone can conduct a funeral ceremony when there is to be a cremation, but if your family member was a member of a faith, then you would expect that the minster of that faith would take the service. For a pagan there are usually several places to find a celebrant and your undertaker should be able to help you with all of this. It is possible, however, that your family member is a Druid, a Wiccan or follows one of the other pagan paths and has requested what is called a 'Natural Burial' or a 'Woodland Burial'.

This takes place out of doors and is a little different from regular services in that the person is buried in place of nature such as a wood. Many official woodland burial sites exist. The service would give you and the family time to say a few words, sing something or have someone sing for you, have your loved one blessed and then placed down into the ground. The people who look after the grounds of the natural burial site will fill the hole in and then replace the grass over the place where the person has been buried. You would not expect many flower arrangements in a natural burial. Everything has to be bio-degradable and tied with grass. And in a natural burial there are usually no grave stones, but sometimes you can plant a tree close to the spot or there may be a wall nearby where a plaque can be put up. It is normally a place that is very like the natural countryside, with trees and bushes, a place where you can return and remember your loved one who has passed on.

A Story: Ashley's Great-Grandma

Ashley was very sad. Her great-grandma was very old, 99 years old to be exact, and she had been looking forward to a card from the Queen, but that was not to be. Last night she had gone to bed, gone to sleep as she always had for the last 99 years, but this time she never woke up.

Grandma and mum were both very sad, but kept saying things like, 'My goodness what a wonderful age', and, 'What a wonderful life she has had'. All of this was true, but still it was very sad to think that great-grandma was not going to get her card from the Queen after all.

Great-grandma had been born in 1913 when things were changing; women had started to cut their hair instead of keeping it long and putting it up into difficult to manage hair styles. And the fashion had changed, although many women still wore corsets and needed someone else to help them dress. Little boys were dressed like little girls until they grew out of nappies and then they had their hair cut for the first time and went into short trousers. Everything was so very different when great-grandma had been born.

When she was 18 years old, great-grandma had married a soldier. He had been injured in the First World War. At that time great-grandma was nursing soldiers and had met and fallen in love with great-granddad.

So for many wonderful years great-grandma had raised a family, survived the Second World War with great-granddad, who never went back into the army because of his previous injuries. They had a lovely house at the edge of the town, within walking distance of the countryside. They had kept dogs, different breeds over the years, and in the end great-grandma gave a home to a stray from the local animal charity. After great-granddad had died this little dog had kept her company for many years, 21 years to be exact! But the little dog had died last year, which had made great-grandma very sad. The little dog had gone to the Summerlands.

I can almost hear you asking, 'Where is the Summerlands?' You would be quite right to ask and I will do what I can to tell you the answer.

The sun comes up here in Europe in the east, it travels across the sky and eventually goes to bed in the west. The west had always been a magical direction to some, the magical god-like folk would travel 'to the west' with the setting sun and you would never see them again unless they came to visit.

The Summerlands is a place where it's nice and warm, it doesn't rain all the time, no one has any pain or illness, no one is unhappy or sad. It is a spiritual place, people go there after they die, they leave their body behind for their family to either bury or cremate and their spirit, the very essence of what makes them who they are, travels on to the west and to the Summerlands.

It's a place where you meet your ancestors. You meet up with those who have already left to go and live there. You can recognise each other, but you don't have a physical body, you are pure spirit, light, energy.

It is said, from a pagan point of view, that our loved ones leave this world and travel to the Summerlands. There they drink from the well of forgetfulness. In other words they forget all the bad and nasty things that have happened in their life on Earth.

So this was where great-grandma had gone. She had left her body in the middle of the night and travelled to the Summerlands to be with her loved ones and her ancestors, Ashley's ancestors.

So while everyone was very sad, and were all going to miss great-grandma a great deal, great-grandma was off with her husband. She would meet up with everyone else who had passed on and no doubt was going to have a party!

So for her it was wonderful. She would not be in pain, have to take any more tablets or have the nurse dress her swollen ankles, she was free; but Ashley and her family were sad, very sad.

About a week after she died they had a service up in the town graveyard, just a brief one with a celebrant who was asked to come along and say a few words. None of the family were religious in the conventional sense, Ashley's family were pagan, spiritual but not religious.

But later that evening all the family came together and formed a circle and Ashley's mum for the first time took control of the ceremony, she spoke directly to great-grandma as if she was still in the room.

She said: 'You have been called to the hall of your ancestors, you have seen many changes, taken many ceremonies yourself, but now you are released from the care and worry of this world. Go with our love and travel quickly and well, we will miss you but we know you are only a thought away just behind the veil. We will call you into our circles at each gathering and we look forward to having you join us from the Summerlands.'

There was a hushed silence as folks tried to stop themselves from crying and thought of all the good times that they had shared with great-grandma. Ashley stayed very quiet. She was not old enough to speak openly in circles.

But then her mother turned around to look at Ashley and asked her if she wanted to say anything, which was a surprise but all she could do was look at the candle burning in the middle of the circle.

The family shared some food, a few sandwiches and fruit juice, with cups of tea, coffee and wine for the adults. Someone had brought a fruit cake and this was cut up and shared. And then most of them went home and Ashley went to bed while her mum and some of the others in the family did the washing up and cleaned up after the gathering.

Over the next few months, it was very clear that although great-grandma had left this world, left her body behind, she was still around. There were little things which made you realise; the painting on the wall which was moved sideways from time to time, the candles that came back to life after they had been put out, the cat which looked into space and then started to purr, lots of little things that made you realise that she was indeed just a thought away, just the other side of an unseen veil.

Great-grandma was still around, but lived in the Summerlands and came to visit when she was asked or at times dropped in to see them. Although not all the family had the gift of being able to see her, the cat certainly could.

Part Three
The Afterlife

The Summerlands, the Other Side, Life after Death

Emanuel Swedenborg, who lived from 1688 to 1772, inspired Andrew Jackson Davis, who lived from 1826 to 1910 and wrote about the Summerlands in his major work *The Great Harmonia*. In it he said that Summerland is the pinnacle of human spiritual achievement in the afterlife; that is, it is the highest level, or 'sphere', of the afterlife we can hope to enter.

C.W. Leadbeater, who was influential in a religion called Theosophy which believed in reincarnation, also taught that those who were good in their previous earthly incarnation went to a place called Summerland between incarnations.

The belief of the afterlife is varied though and not all pagans believe in the same thing. There appear to be two main beliefs. The first is reincarnation, that after life we are reborn as another human, or perhaps an animal. The second, which has more historic support (there are records stating this is what the ancient Druids believed in) is that we go to the Otherworld after death. The Otherworld is a place where both the good and the bad go, a place where we live a spiritual life.

The ancient peoples of Ireland and Britain mourned a birth because to them in a sense it meant someone had died in the Otherworld to have a new life in the physical. They also celebrated deaths because it meant a birth in the Otherworld.

Belief in some kind of life after this one, life after death, is a very personal thing. Some may refer to it as 'the next life', others give it a name, Summerlands, Heaven, Valhalla, Annwen, to name just a few. But if you were to ask a pagan, most would believe in some form of existence in spirit form after this physical life.

For me, as for many other pagan folk, I would call it the Summerlands, a place where we go to meet up with our ancestors, our family and our deities. It is somewhere that our spirit can rest, be refreshed and be nourished in the love of all those who are already in the Summerlands. But what of other pagan paths?

Those following a Norse, or heathen, tradition may speak of Valhalla, the hall of the slain, the place where all the champions go if they fall in battle. This must be a very large hall, considering all the deaths there have been over the centuries in battles and wars! To die fighting for your tribe, or your country, in an effort to protect the weak would certainly suggest a place in Valhalla.

But there are other places for the Norse followers to go and not all of them appear to be very nice. Freya chooses some of the slain to live in her halls. In particular she is said to choose fierce independent women. 'Hel', which is a covered hall, would be the place where many others would go to. It is a hall where those who may not have died in battle go to meet up with their ancestors and loved ones. It is somewhere they will be nourished in a spiritual manner.

But there is yet another place for heathens to go to after they die, 'Nifhel'. This is a dark or misty hall where those who have broken an oath go after they die. It seems that to be apart from ones loved ones, not being able to meet with our ancestors, would indeed be a dark place to be.

The ancient Egyptians also believed in a life after death. In fact they spent a great deal of effort making sure their next life was a good one. Life in this world had to be lived in harmony with 'Maat', which was the ancient Egyptian concept of truth, balance, order, law, morality, and justice. Maat was also personified as a goddess regulating the stars, seasons, and the actions of both mortals and the deities who set the order of the universe from chaos at the moment of creation.

In order to be sure of a good afterlife, having lived a life in harmony with all that was required, a person's spirit was then weighed by Osiris after death. If it was found to be acceptable they were then permitted to travel to the Otherworld in a peaceful and serene manner and live among the deities and their ancestors. They might become stars in the night sky!

Those who follow a Celtic path could historically be from several different tribes of the Gaels or British, such as Welsh or Scottish, and from parts of the western side of England. These days, with so many people having settled in other parts of the world, there are those following a Celtic path in the US, in New Zealand and in Australia, possibly anywhere in the world where people from Ireland and Britain have settled. Some of them would have different names for the afterlife. The Welsh sometimes speak of 'Annwm' or 'Anmwfn' and many others talk of the Summerlands.

In the case of those who follow a Celtic pagan path, they almost always believe in a life after death. They would see this as a spiritual life, a place where they can rest and learn. Many will believe in reincarnation after a time of rest.

In other words, they feel that after a period of time spent in the spirit lands, the Summerlands, they are offered another life and if they choose can start again with a new baby body and have the chance to learn even more in the next incarnation.

If you can imagine a large tree, it grows leaves in the spring and all through the year those leaves live on the tree. Come the autumn, if this is the kind of tree that loses its leaves each year, then they will fall and die. But the tree is not dead and the next year new leaves will grow again from the same tree.

The belief that there is a part of you which travels to the Otherworld, or the Summerlands, and then after a while gets a chance to be born again as a baby to live another life and to learn again, is reincarnation. It's the rebirth of that spiritual part of you and this can happen many, many different times.

From a nursing point of view, being a retired nurse myself, if anyone died in our ward a window was left open if possible, or a door. The person was laid down and then left for about an hour for the spirit of the person to have a clear time in which to leave. After that we would go back into the room and wash the body very carefully and make them look presentable for any family who wished to come to say goodbye.

A Story: A Summerland Dream

Mrs Richardson, Cathy to her friends, was very tired. She had been teaching all day and her pupils had been asking all kinds of questions, some she just couldn't answer. She got home, made herself a cup of tea with two sugars, took her shoes off and went to sit down in her comfortable chair in her sitting room. She was just going to have half an hour rest before starting on her chores. The washing that had been hanging up on a dryer all day needed ironing and she needed to make preparations for her dinner.

Mr Richardson was away on a job. He worked on an oil rig in the North Sea and was away from home for several weeks at a time, but then he did have weeks at home.

Their children were all grown up now. One was at college, one was at university and one of them had joined the Navy and had been learning all kinds of interesting things. So the whole house was quiet, peaceful, which was wonderful because Cathy Richardson's day had been spent with some very noisy and lively ten-year-olds at school.

Within a few moments she had drifted off into a kind of half sleep, completely relaxed yet not fully asleep and then she saw some people in her dream...

'We've been waiting for you, we can help you answer some of your pupils' questions,' said a group of very normal looking folk, ranging from teenagers to much older but very bright and upright people.

They were waiting on a path in the sunshine. Surrounding them was countryside and buildings in the distance.

'Come with us and we can show you around,' said one of them.

Cathy was surprised, but thought it was worth a visit, so off they went chatting away about the weather and what they had been doing today. One said she had been having violin lessons from a master player, another said she was so pleased to be able to learn how to paint. Another said she had been growing herbs and gathering seeds to give to her friends.

'Where are we?' asked Cathy.

'You have come for a visit to the Summerlands, but you can only stay very briefly,' replied one of the people.

'Here we are,' they said and proceeded to show her into a large hall that looked like an open-air chamber. All around them were groups of people. Many smiled and a few waved and nodded, yet overhead there was no roof, and Cathy looked up. Her confusion must have shown in the expression on her face because one of the group said, 'It's always warm and sunny, it never rains or snows. We don't need a ceiling.'

'What are we waiting for?' asked Cathy.

'Arrivals,' one said.

And then almost as soon as they had said that a few people started to walk through the door at the far end of the hall. As they came forward, different groups moved towards them, greeted them and took them off out of the hall and over to sit on the grass to chat for a while.

Some walked forward looking a little dazed and a couple of tall people, dressed in white, came forward and took them off through another door, they seemed to glide away.

'Where have the shining people taken them?' asked Cathy.

'These are people who are shocked, they need to rest and they are going over to the resting area. Come we will show you.'

And they all moved through the door towards the resting area to find what looked like an outdoor hospital, with raised beds but without a bed frame, all covered in a soft white material. People were lying asleep on the beds and tall, shining people were gliding up and down the aisles between the beds checking each person, putting a hand on a brow or a hand on a shoulder and watching them carefully.

'They are healing,' said one of the group.

This then was a healing centre and the people who were looking after the patients were healers. Everyone was resting and healing, ready to go off and join their group of ancestors.

At the top of the healing hospital there was a large stone well, and in this was water, it was a clear blue colour. Every now and then one of the healers would go and fetch a drink of this water from the well and take it to patients who were stirring, for them to sip at the cool water.

'What's in the stone container?' asked Cathy.

'This is the Well of Forgetfulness,' said one of the group. They went on to explain that some of the people who were healing had experienced terrible things before they came there. A drink from the well would help them forget all the nasty terrible happenings and allow them to start to heal in this world.

The group moved on and found what looked like a play school, with little children running around and playing. There were lots of healers here too, but these all had aprons on and some were pushing prams around the edge of the area.

'These are children who have arrived without their own parents,' one of the group said.

Just as she said that a much older lady with grey hair tied up in a bun arrived to collect one of the children.

'Yes, this is one of mine,' said the older lady and carried the little child off, kissing it and cuddling it all the time.

Cathy looked at her guides for an explanation and was told that these were great-grandmas, some of them were great-great-great-grandmas, whose role it was to look after any of the little ones from their descendants. They grew up and were taught here in the open air and when they were old enough had the chance of going back to one of their family for another chance.

Cathy was starting to feel very heavy and the group looked at each other and nodded. 'You can't stay for much longer, this is only a visit to help you teach your children in your school, you can't stay with us for a long time yet,' said one of the guides.

With that they took her over the countryside, their feet never seemed to touch the floor and it was as if they were gliding a few inches above the ground. All of a sudden they were back where Cathy had been when she first arrived in this place.

'Thank you so much,' said Cathy. She turned to shake hands with some of her guides, but they had started to fade and then they were gone.

The clock in the hall of Cathy Richardson's house struck six. She had been asleep or in a dream-like state for much longer than she had thought, but as she opened her eyes and looked around her she saw everything was exactly as she had left it, except that her tea was now cold.

Little by little Cathy remembered all about her trip, about the people she had met and all she had learnt and knew now that some questions the children had asked could be answered.

The Summerlands was a warm, sunny place, there were healers and people to help. Your family came to meet you, but if you were hurt, tired or something nasty had happened, then there were healers in the spirit world and everyone was taken care of. Children grew up there, and great-grandmas who were already there came and collected little children and took them off to their family to be loved and cared for.

Cathy went into her kitchen to make a new cup of tea for herself and said in a loud voice, 'Thank you for your help.'

The voice of one of her guides was heard to say, 'You are most welcome!'

Conclusion

In this book I have introduced a range of ideas about deity, gods from different lands and different times. Many of these ancient gods are followed in the modern pagan community. The rituals that are used to honour these deities may be very different from the rituals used in ancient times, but the intent behind them is very similar. People of the past were trying to make sense of the world around them and wanted to connect with beings they felt could bring some order to their lives. They were trying to communicate with beings they couldn't see or touch. Modern pagans have a different understanding of what causes many of the wonders in the world around us, but we still seek to develop relationships with beings we cannot usually see or touch either.

I moved on to talk about rites of passage; ways in which we mark major events in our lives. People throughout history and across the world will have used special ceremonies to mark significant events in their lives. Every community I know regardless of what faith has similar special ceremonies to mark significant events. Ceremonies like these are some of the ways we build relationships with each other in our communities.

Finally, I talked about the afterlife and introduced one common pagan view of it as well as touching on some other pagan ideas. Most religions have a view that life is more than what we can see and touch in everyday reality. Most faiths will have ideas about the afterlife. One thing that I think they hold in common is that we all wish for a happy afterlife both for ourselves and those we love. Our communities may have different ideas on what will make us happy, but we share that desire for happiness in my opinion. One of the reasons that we think about an afterlife is that even though someone is dead we still want to have a relationship of some kind with them.

It is my hope that in writing this book I will help others to understand a little more of the ways in which pagans develop relationships with their gods, with each other and how they continue to relate to those who have died.

Children in particular seem to enjoy stories that give them examples of how things might work and activities that they can try for themselves. Many faiths in the modern world have sacred books that include many such stories. Paganism does not have a single sacred book to refer to and not many of the pagan books that are around are aimed at both children and their parents and teachers.

Within the pagan faith there are some ancient myths and other stories written by early writers who have gathered together stories passed down by word of mouth. Some writers will have written things down without changing what they heard while others will have written extra bits or taken bits they didn't like out for many different reasons. What is encouraged within the pagan faith is that people find their own path, that they keep notes, read a little about different aspects of paganism and find the one which draws them. Sometimes this has to do with their background, their ancestors, or simply that they are looking for the god they feel is accessible to them. Sometimes this process does not begin until an individual is an adult, but it can start for those at a younger age. This book introduces ideas and activities that will help children think about paganism and concepts such as deity, rites of passage and afterlife in other faiths too.

One idea that can be introduced at a very young age regardless of faith is a love of nature, a respect for creation and an understanding that this has evolved over thousands and thousands of years. Following on from this respect for the world we live on comes a need to help the planet in every way possible. The simplest would perhaps be to recycle. Happily many schools and homes now do recycle as much as they can. We need to teach our children this respect and start from an early age.

In addition to helping children learn respect for the world around them, we also need to help them learn to respect other people about them. Our modern world is one of near instant communication from one side of the world to the other. We are bombarded with images of different peoples, different cultures and different ways of doing things. We can either react to these things with fear or with compassion and respect. Whatever our faith, we have more in common with each other as individual people than many of us remember. The details of our ceremonies and rituals may vary tremendously but at their heart is the need to build relationships with both each other and the unseen world around us.

Afterword: For Parents and Teachers Using This Book

It is my hope that this book will be used in schools as a resource for comparative religious studies as well as by parents who wish to help their own children learn about paganism. With that in mind I offer these final thoughts and suggestions.

To use this book as a teaching aid, I would suggest that having first read it through and got an understanding of the subject matter from a Wiccan/ pagan point of view, you then take a chapter that relates to your particular needs at that time and do some or all of the following:

- Read the chapter again and make some notes, check online for further details about this aspect.
- Either read the story to your children or class or, if you feel the children could read it themselves, then allow them to do this and then afterwards discuss the story with them.
- Ask the children to either collect items or draw items relating to the story. Depending on what chapter is chosen this could be further enhanced with a visit to a museum, an ancient site or another religious venue.
- Round the chapter off by getting the children to tell you and each other how a modern pagan might feel about the area you are focussing on. Try to help the children understand how a modern pagan might view it.
- Share some snacks, or make something which relates to the whole chapter.

In the Rites of Passage section I have written a simple play that the children can act out to demonstrate marriage or handfasting and I hope you find this of use.

It can be difficult to talk to children about death and the afterlife and it may be necessary to find out before you introduce this topic if anyone in your group has recently lost a member of the family or a friend. Depending on what the circumstances are, you may wish to tailor what you include accordingly.

Stories and other forms of art are good ways for children to display their feelings about death and hopefully the story about the Summerlands will give them some idea of a place where it's warm, sunny; a place where people are not suffering any longer. Remind the children that you can still talk about loved ones who have died even if it makes you sad sometimes. From a pagan point of view, and indeed that of many other faiths, they will meet up with them again one day.

Bibliography and Further Notes

I have used several books and websites to help in writing this book and these are some of them:

The Pagan Religions of the Ancient British Isles by Ronald Hutton
Norse Mythology by John Lindow
The Road to Hel by Hilda Roderick Ellis M.A. Ph.D.
Wikipedia.
www.bbc.co.uk/food/recipes
Encyclopedia of World Mythology by Arthur Cotterell
Encyclopedia of Gods by Michael Jordan
Readers Digest Complete Wordfinder
Circle Round: Raising Children in Goddess Traditions by Starhawk
The Complete Book of Incense, Oils and Brews by Scott Cunningham
Agreed Syllabus for Religious Education (England and Wales)
www.eriding.net

Appendix: Notes on the Education (Scotland) Act and Additional Resources

The Education (Scotland) Act states that: 'Religious and moral education includes learning about Christianity, Islam and other world religions, and supports the development of beliefs and values.'

From this one would conclude that learning and supporting the beliefs and values of other faiths, including pagan, should also fit into this. Although at this stage it does not state such a point. It is to be hoped that those teachers who find they do in fact have children from pagan parents in their class would attempt to support them, and use the opportunity to teach the class a little about their faith.

Additional resources

http://www.pookapages.com/ Resources aimed at pagan children
http://www.scottishinterfaithcouncil.org/resources/VALUES+IN+HARMONY.pdf
Values in Harmony outlines the core ethical and moral values held in common across 11 faith and belief communities.

9781780999456